BLUE BARRY BEAR COUNTS FROM 1 TO 20

By Marilyn Sadler
Illustrated by Roger Bollen

A GOLDEN BOOK • NEW YORK
Western Publishing Company, Inc., Racine, Wisconsin 53404

"What a good boy!" said Blue Barry Bear's
mother one day. Blue Barry had just learned
to count from one to twenty.

"Can I go visit Grandma and Grandpa?" he
asked. "I want to show them how far I can count."

"Of course you may," answered his mother.
"But first you must eat your breakfast."

"One," said Blue Barry as he ate one big bowl of cereal.

1

"Two," said Blue Barry as he drank two glasses of orange juice.

3 "Three," said Blue Barry as he ate three blueberry muffins.

The only thing Blue Barry liked better than counting was eating.

Blue Barry counted everything on the way to his grandparents' house. He counted four balloons being carried by one funny bunny.

4

5 He tiptoed past five deer resting quietly in a field.

He waved hello to a family of ducks on the river. He counted one mother duck and six babies.

6

7 He stopped in the middle of a grassy meadow and watched seven squirrels eating eight acorns. **8**

Blue Barry couldn't look anywhere at anything without counting what he saw. He counted nine tall, thin trees as he passed them along the road.

10 He counted ten bluebirds on a telephone wire, singing a lovely song.

He counted eleven fluffy clouds in the sky.
One cloud reminded him of Grandpa.

11

12 And when he came upon twelve angry bees, Blue Barry counted every one of them as he hurried on his way.

Finally, even Blue Barry got tired, and he sat down to rest.

But while he was resting he couldn't stop counting. He counted thirteen very busy ants.

14 He counted fourteen jumping frogs.

He counted fifteen beautiful butterflies. **15**

16

And once Blue Barry was on his way again, he counted sixteen pink flowers in a field.

Blue Barry was very tired when he finally got to his grandparents' house. He didn't even notice there were seventeen pickets in their fence...

18
or eighteen stones in their sidewalk...

or nineteen apples in their tree. **19**

Grandma and Grandpa were very happy to see Blue Barry. "You're just in time for milk and cookies!" Grandma exclaimed.

Blue Barry was tired. But he couldn't wait to show his grandparents how he had learned to count to twenty.

So he counted twenty of Grandma's delicious chocolate chip cookies...

as he ate them one at a time.